the
humble
art of
zen-cleansing
by michael de jong

clean

joost elffers books

CLEAN
The Humble Art of Zen-Cleansing
A Joost Elffers Production

Copyright © 2005 by Michael de Jong and Joost Elffers Books
Text © 2005 by Michael de Jong
All rights reserved.
Published by Joost Elffers Books, LLC.
New York, NY
Design by Yumi Asai at Berrymatch LLC.
Library of Congress data available
ISBN 0-9718975-1-4
10 9 8 7 6 5 4 3 2 1   06 07 08 09 10
Printed in China

....

"CLEAN" is dedicated to my Richard,

who I can bet will probably never use this book.

Acknowledgments

"CLEAN" would not have been possible were it not for the suggestions, support, encouragement, and talents of the following people who I want to thank from the bottom of my heart:

My mom, Ruth De Jong

My brother, John, and twin sister Mags

My partner for life, Richard Haymes

Matthew Waldman and his talented design team at Berrymatch

The incomparable Joost Elffers, my publisher and friend, and the anonymous cab driver who brought us together.

Index

	baking soda	borax	lemon	salt	white vinegar	pages
Cutting board			x	x		68·82
D						
Decking: weathering	x					41
Deodorant residue					x	112
Diaper pail	x					39
Disinfectant		x				63
Dishwasher					x	101
Dishwasher soap	x	x			x	116
Dishes					x	98·110
Dog bedding	x					50
Drain opener	x				x	116
Drains				x		79
Driveway oil	x					51
E						
Enamel	x					39
Electric dishwasher soap	x	x			x	116
Electric iron					x	92

	baking soda	borax	lemon	salt	white vinegar	pages
O						
Onion odor	x		x	x		37·117
Oven					x	103
Oven cleaner	x		x			117
Oven spill				x		76
P						
Paint brushes					x	92
Paint odors					x	110
Pans	x	x	x	x	x	64·102·123
Patent leather					x	91
Pantyhose				x		82
Pet urine					x	94
Perspiration stains	x					39
Plastic toys	x					46
Pressing creases					x	92
Porcelain	x		x			39·123
Pots		x	x		x	64·72·102

x

	baking soda	borax	lemon	salt	white vinegar	pages
Shoes: deodorize	x					54
Shower curtain				x	x	79·113
Shower doors					x	105
Shower stall					x	105
Silk flowers				x		84
Silver	x					56
Skunk odors					x	96
Skin softener	x					49
Smoke					x	95·104
Smoke damage	x		x		x	121
Spot remover			x	x		123
Soap film					x	89
Soap scum					x	105
Soapsuds removal				x		81
Stainless steel	x				x	39·101
Static cling					x	91
Stuffed Animals	x					46
Surface cleaner	x					39

Preface

In 1987 I moved to New York to become an artist. I had just finished graduate school and had high hopes and expectations of what life as an artist in New York City might be like. Thank God I was so naive or I might not have done it in the first place. With a cat and a single piece of luggage filled to capacity, I surprisingly found a small apartment on the lower east side, just off the Bowery. I set up a little studio in the apartment and began making work. Even more surprisingly, I found a gallery to exhibit in (and another to be the Director of) in record time. My first one-person show opened just five months after I arrived in NY, and after plenty of sales and promising reviews, I quit my full-time job to become an Artist.

That was also when I began cleaning apartments for extra cash to supplement my income from the sales of my art. I'd never done this before, but my plan allowed me to paint in the morning and to clean in the afternoon. I placed an ad in the *Village Voice* advertising myself as a male housekeeper who cleaned "In the European Tradition" —whatever that meant. But it sounds convincing, doesn't it? Forty-five responses from the ad offered me a solid group of people to interview. I set up appointments carrying an attaché case (empty of course) and wearing a crisp shirt and tie to meet clients and see which homes were, in fact, the smallest and easiest to clean. I probably don't need to tell you that most of the responses were from whackos and freaks. It is New York after all. One prospective client actually greeted me at his door naked and tried to encourage me to join him in his newfound nudist freedom.

In the end I managed to find only four individuals who were sincere—and infinitely cleaner than I would ever dream of being. And so I began traveling the subways from the Cloisters to the World Trade Center, going from apartment to apartment with a homemade cleaning kit of commercially manufactured scouring powders and surface cleaners, paper towels, garbage bags, rags and whatnot. I wasn't sure of what I needed, or frankly of what I was doing, but as a child I had watched my mom wash and vacuum the floor, wipe down the counters, and scour the bathroom. Since I had inherited her addiction to cleanliness and used it in my college dorm rooms and now my own NYC hovel, I figured I could do it for others.

I cleaned with abandon. Bleach infused powder filled the air while I sprayed grease cutting agents to quickly clean, deodorize and disinfect. Glass cleaners hovered and oven cleaners fumed as I vacuumed, laundered, wiped and polished. The windows shined and surfaces sparkled. Beds had military corners and dust bunnies were exterminated. Closets were organized, and slipcovers, walls and even lampshades were restored to their original cleanliness. The effect was dazzling.

I, however, felt like hell. It was then that I came to realize that the overexposure to household cleaning products was robbing me of my health.

Since I couldn't afford to quit, I needed a solution, and this is how I came by it. I began to consider that, perhaps, cleaning products needn't always come from the hardware or grocery store. Pioneers traveled across the plains without handy wipes, dishwasher tabs or self-sanitizing lotion. And had it not been for the fact that they were probably trampled by their own livestock, killed by each other, or didn't pack enough rations for their travels, most would have arrived at their destination, hardy, healthy and clean.

No matter how you look at it, cleaning is hard work. I'm not going to tell you I have a magic solution that will make cleaning a breeze. And there are certainly ways of making any cleaning chore easier, but using commercial cleaning products is not the solution. These may work well on your counter top—but they could also send you into cardiac arrest. And honestly, they don't actually work so well. After seven years of cleaning professionally, I can attest to that. Now I have come to think that cleaning with wholesome ingredients is not an alternative but the solution. It's cheaper, healthier, easier, and it's infinitely more effective.

CLEAN (The Humble Art of Zen-Cleansing)
…or how to become your own cleaning Buddhist.

"Cleanliness is indeed next to godliness."

(John Wesley)

Okay, the truth of the matter is most people hate to clean. It's a necessary evil, and even then most find ways of avoiding it -- or simply get someone else to do it for them. However, I'll admit to being the weirdo in the crowd who, on many levels, truly enjoys cleaning.

I actually move the fridge when I vacuum. Not what the average housekeeper might do, but that's just me. (It's a little obsessive, I admit—OK, a lot obsessive—but you'd be surprised what you find missing, or worse yet, lurking there.) Mine is a cleaning ritual I learned from my Dutch-born mother, Ruth, and by doing it I gain peace of mind—the satisfaction of knowing that my kitchen is really clean.

My mom was my cleaning Guru! My devotion to and gratification from cleaning I owe to her. And it all surely started with the "Cleaning Game" she played with my siblings and me every Saturday morning when we were young. She somehow got us to eagerly pick three to four "special chores" from a bowl to finish before playtime. Over the years, cleaning became ingrained in me as an inspirational, almost spiritual-like exercise that brings self-satisfaction as well as happiness to those around us.

As a result, every day, I make it a habit to do just a little cleaning before leaving for work. But on Saturdays I spin like some caffeinated twister shaking rugs 'til the bindings come loose, vacuuming until the machine gags from lack of suction, washing shirts that are actually going to the professional laundry on Monday, changing beds (including two guest beds whether we've had company or not), scrubbing out the sinks, tubs and toilets, and mopping every square inch of my living space, which I share with a partner who does not have my passion for cleaning. I admit it, were I the type to have a housekeeper, I would probably clean before he or she arrived.

Occasionally my intense focus and energy succeeds in frightening my partner into a state of suspension in which he hypnotically offers his acquiescent assistance and gets caught up in my transcendental cleansing enterprises. But most times he just finds reasons to leave the house altogether—to go grocery shopping or, with our dog Jack in tow, take an extended visit to the park and local coffee shop until "it's over."

But again, that's just me. I expect this of no one. So please don't panic. This book is not about cleaning obsessions—to the contrary, it's about the mindfulness of cleaning effectively with the simplest and safest of ingredients. It's about doing what most people hate in a way that is actually healthful, thoughtful and respectful—of yourself, your loved ones, your pets and neighbors, your environment, and your planet.

In essence, this book is about what I irreverently call "Zen-Cleansing." Many religious philosophies respect cleanliness and the act of cleaning—it's "next to Godliness" and all that. And if you think about it, it is in our spiritual nature to pursue some level of cleanliness and order. Faiths such as Islam, Christianity, Judaism, Buddhism and Hinduism have age-old parables that speak of the humility and spiritual importance in washing, organization and other household activities.

For instance, the closer a Buddhist comes to being one with the Universe, the more menial his or her daily tasks become. The highest-ranking monks are given the honor of cleaning up after meals. (Wow, imagine if our highest-ranking politicians and CEO's behaved similarly—actually serving citizens and consumers!) It is a Zen Buddhist spiritual goal to create inner and outward purity by achieving inner and universal harmony through applying care and mindfulness to everyday, lowly activities as if they actually mattered.

From this simple, yet somewhat difficult practice, it is implied that by cleaning with care we can allow the task to become a meaningful, transcendental experience. I must admit that in my Whirling Dervish Saturday cleaning spurts, my head is cleared, and my body and mind feel harmonized—that's why I call it "Zen-Cleansing."

Zen-Cleansing is a mindful way of letting go of the drudgery associated with cleaning, and finding your spick and span center-

-to joyously give yourself up to cleaning. Not just spritzing, wiping, soaking, scrubbing, scouring, vacuuming, mopping, dusting, and shining…but rather spritzing, wiping, soaking, scrubbing, scouring, vacuuming, mopping, dusting, and shining with a concern for and a knowing oneness with the Universe!

Some Eastern philosophies teach us that the Universe is controlled by the interaction of the elements, and when paired with the duality of the ying and the yang, create contrast, tension, conflict and balance. Much like the five elements in Chinese medicine (wood, fire, earth, metal, water) and the five elements in Asian cooking (sour, bitter, sweet, spicy, salty), there are five elements in Zen-Cleansing and they also operate on the same principles. In Zen-Cleansing, all elements are equally important. They depend on one another for an amazing chain of reaction-interaction. It is the pairing, marriage and balance that make for the spiritual, integrated experience. Each ingredient has its own place and each has its own function—both singularly and in combination with the others.

The five simple ingredients that are used in Zen-Cleansing are baking soda, borax, lemon, salt, and white vinegar. There is nothing new or unusual about any of them, and in fact, they have been used for centuries. I would wager that at least four if not all five ingredients are already in your home. They are pure, wholesome and natural—and none will hurt (and may actually help!) you, your family, your pets, your neighborhood or the environment.

What is truly amazing about these simple ingredients is that their combinations create catalysts for cleanliness. When a sodium substance such as the salt, borax or baking soda is exposed to an acid substance such as the white vinegar or lemon, carbon dioxide—CO_2—is released. Carbon dioxide in its solid form is better known as dry ice. But no need to worry, by mixing any of the five Zen-Cleansing agents, you will never create dry ice in your home. Don't expect to see the pillows of puffy white clouds or spooky smoky tendrils you remember from your childhood when the science teacher put a chunk in a bowl of water. And there is no need to worry about touching any of the mixtures—they cannot burn your skin the way dry ice can.

Expect something much more subtle but no less wondrous. In Zen-Cleansing, when any of the salt and acid ingredients are joined and create carbon dioxide, miraculously surfaces are caused to cool ever so slightly and the dirt actually pops off. Carbon dioxide, as the waste product of the joining of the salty and acidic ingredients, provides continuing energy for breaking down sugars and fats with oxygen. I'm not "Mr. Wizard," but that's really the simplest explanation. And regardless of the chemistry, it works.

The ancient Greeks in their wisdom and even the early American colonists in their struggles to survive cleaned with these same basic elements—salt and acid. So, perhaps in this modern age, when new toxic and wasteful cleaning products are introduced to the market on a daily basis (mindlessly enticing us with infomercials and product placements), it's a timely idea for us to rethink using them. After all, it's our homes, our health and our environment we're trying to keep clean. Dogen, a thirteenth century Buddhist teacher taught that any unused water should be returned to the stream that it came from. And any water used while Zen-Cleansing can actually be returned to the environment because the five ingredients—baking soda, borax, lemon, salt, and white vinegar—are completely safe. They harm nothing. They just clean. They are so safe, in fact, that you probably eat four of the five—baking soda, lemon, salt, and vinegar, —on a daily basis. (And just in case I need to remind you, please don't eat the fifth—borax. It's a mineral mined from the ground that, while not biologically harmful, has absolutely no dietary value!)

Unlike today's marketed cleansers, Zen-Cleansing ingredients will not harm your respiratory system, make you cough, give you a bloody nose, loosen your bowels, give you the gout, or leave a poisonous gritty or oily residue on your kitchen or bath surfaces. They will not pollute the air, rivers or soil. Make no mistake, they will require the same "elbow grease" as commercial products, but they won't harm your hands, eyes, lungs, etc., and you won't need rubber gloves to avoid caustic burns. Of course, if you are the type who likes to clean in rubber gloves, by all means, go ahead.

Another thing to note is that unlike commercial products that line the supermarket shelves in colorful and alluring packaging, Zen-Cleansing ingredients will require only some simple packaging that you'll need to supply yourself. The empty plastic spray bottles, peanut butter or mayonnaise jars (that you probably already have or perhaps might even "rescue" from a neighbor's recycling bin) will work perfectly. In fact, just by involving yourself in this simple mindful re-cycling act alone, think of all of the plastic packaging that will no longer need to be manufactured and thus won't find its non-biodegradable way into landfills or recycling centers across the country.

So in addition to being a simple and effective way to clean the toughest dirt, Zen-Cleansing is also an environmentally sane alternative to the prepackaged goods in grocery and hardware stores. Just look through your pantry and refrigerator for what you'll need—you probably already have most of the items on hand. Just think, if we don't buy store-bought toxic cleaning products, then we won't use them. And if we don't use them there's no real reason to make them. The reality is that we really didn't need any of them in the first place, but we've been brainwashed into thinking that we did.

Having said all that, Zen-Cleansing is a philosophy, a kit and a book about cleaning that might just start a revolution. Maybe it's how we reclaim the environment, put big business in its place, and make it safe again not just for our children, loved ones and pets, but for everything that climbs and crawls, flies or swims. Think of it as a way of being one with the Universe on a daily basis, and doing your part to make the world a safer, cleaner, more beautiful place.

The birds in the sky and the fish in the depths of the ocean leave no trace of their passing (OK, they do poop, and sometimes on us!)—and we should take note. In essence your mind and your environment are one. Open your awareness to your actions to benefit the good of every other thing. In Zen, we meet ourselves in whatever task we take on. Whatever we see, whatever we hear, whatever we smell, taste or touch, we end up experiencing as ourselves. In Zen-Cleansing, we meet ourselves in the mindful act of safely and purely cleaning our personal environment.

Your environment, your daily activities and your inner thoughts are one and tell the world who you are…even if you are a messed up, cleaning-obsessed freak like me. So let us wield our cleaning cloths with honor. Refrigerator-movers of the world unite!

[And, dear reader, although cleaning is never "easy," I've made accessing and finding cleaning recipes and "How To's" a lot easier with a handy, user-friendly Index at the beginning of this book.]

baking soda

Introduction to Baking Soda

Fresh from the box, its finely formed crystals sparkle like a freshly fallen first snow. White, powdery and soft to the touch, odorless and inert upon inspection, the lonely baking soda loiters endlessly in the fridge, in the shadows behind leftovers, lunchmeat and lettuce.

From the ashes of burnt corncob, pioneers made early baking sodas named saleratus, trona or nitre. Found on the shelves of frontier homes as well as in the traveling Medicine Man's bag of talismans and herbs, it was prescribed as a cure for everything from asthma to eczema and bellyaches. It transformed animal fat into treatments for chapped skin and did double duty to clean floors, scrub pots, and shine shoes.

Cleaning and bathing with baking soda goes back to biblical times. "For though thou wash with nitre, and take thee much soap, yet thine iniquity is marked before me, saith the Lord God." Jeremiah 2:22. Perhaps implying that even with soap and ash as our purifiers, only God can wash away our transgressions. (I wonder if subconsciously that's why Charles Manson and his followers hid at the Barker Ranch in a town called Trona, California.)

Found in the Valley of the Kings and used by the ancient Egyptians famous for the art of mummification, the key ingredient in the process was nitre or baking soda. Superior as a drying agent because it attacks and destroys grease and fat, it's found not only in tombs but also as residue in the mummies themselves. Established in the beds of Egyptian lakes, the nitre crystals form when water in the heated desert climate evaporates. Traded for thousands of years, Egyptian writings as old as the reign of Ramses III refer to these deposits.

Sprinkled, scattered, spread or strewn, kept in either your closet, kitty litter, crisper or carport, baking soda, in any of its namesakes is powerful enough to preserve the dead. (Not a "do-it-yourself" project!) And yet, it also possesses equal sensitivity to sweeten, clean and freshen your home. Baking soda is the most effective, most useful and most used in the family of five ingredients.

Zen-Cleansing with Baking Soda

- Baking soda works great in the **freezer**, in the **refrigerator**, and in your **closet** to keep it fresh. Just tear the top off a fresh box and let it do its thing. After a month, replace the old baking soda with a fresh one and use the old box in a cleaning project to dispose of it. You can also pour some down your drain to keep it free of odors.

• Try spot cleaning **wallpaper** by making a paste of baking soda and water. (A paste may be made by adding a few drops of water to a quarter cup of baking soda. The finished product should resemble the consistency of toothpaste.) Wipe on with a soft cloth and attempt to remove the soil or spot in a slow, methodical circular motion. Follow by wiping again with a clean, lightly dampened cloth. This will require a delicate hand, some patience, and the ability to say, "Enough is enough."

• By adding baking soda to your **scouring pad**, you may prevent it from rusting.

• Place musty **books**, old or new, into a plastic bag with baking soda to eliminate mildew and stinky odors. Allow it to absorb the odors and mildew (or until the offending smell has disappeared.) The process may take a few weeks.

• To rid your **hands** of **odors**, like onions or even garlic, quickly scrub with baking soda and water. Use a nailbrush, if you think you need to, and then rinse with warm running water.

• For tough surface stains, in a medium bowl, add one half box and enough water to get baking soda the consistency of cake batter. Use it to scour **tiles**, **fiberglass**, **fine china**, **porcelain**, **enameled surfaces**, **stainless steel**, **aluminum** and even **cast iron**. Scrub, rinse and wipe dry. The scouring mixture should keep for a few days if stored in a covered airtight container.

• Make a baking soda and water paste and rub it into a **perspiration stain**. Really unfortunate stains may need to sit for an hour or two. Wash as usual.

• A cup of baking soda sprinkled into your **baby's diaper pail** will keep it smelling fresh (er?).

- Zap away **microwave stains**. Put two or three spoons of baking soda into one cup of water and boil it for two minutes in your microwave. The steam from the boiling baking-soda-infused water will soften even the hardest, greasy, yucky, baked on messes. Wipe clean.

- A paste of baking soda and water is gentle enough to remove **shoe** and **furniture scuffs** on all kinds of flooring.

- Sprinkle baking soda to absorb even your greasiest stains on **fabric** and **silk** upholstery. Don't work it in but just let it sit overnight and then vacuum the baking soda up.

- Add two cups of baking soda to a gallon of water to give a new **deck** a weathered look instantly.

- Add one half of a cup of baking soda to a bucket of water to **mop floors**. Mop as usual, rinse and wipe dry.

- Place a cup of baking soda every week down your toilet or drain to help maintain the PH balance of your septic **tank** and to keep it flowing smoothly.

- Rinse **pesticides**, **dirt** and **wax** from fruit and vegetables by adding a few tablespoons of baking soda to a sink of warm water. Rinse with clean water, pat dry, display and, of course, devour.

• Remove **scratches** and **cuts** from **laminated counters** by cleaning with a baking soda-water paste. Rub in circular motion and watch them disappear. Be prepared to contribute some elbow grease.

• Remove **ink stains** on **countertops** from price tags or plastic bags with a baking soda and water paste. For old or stubborn stains, apply lemon juice first.

• Make a **tile cleaner** that will remove even tough **mildew stains** by mixing two cups of baking soda and a half-cup of lukewarm water. Use an old toothbrush or household brush to work it into the grout and scrub, scrub, scrub. Rinse with warm water.

- Sprinkle a fresh **mud spot** on your **carpet** or **rugs** with enough baking soda to cover it completely. Let stand for 20 minutes and then vacuum.

- Similarly, cover **grease spots** in your rug with baking soda. Let it sit for one hour, scrub with a dry brush and then vacuum.

- If your **carpets** and **rugs** smell musty, sprinkle a thin layer of baking soda over the entire surface. Let sit overnight, and then vacuum.

- Remove **bloodstains** from color-safe **fabrics** by rinsing them with cold water, then sprinkle on baking soda. Rub the fabric into itself and run under cool water again.

Vacuum 'til the cord tells you to stop.

45

- To clean your child's **stuffed animals**, pour a cup of baking soda into a large, clean plastic bag. Place the toys into the bag and shake. Remove the toys and shake them over the garbage can to remove the remaining powder. Vacuum if necessary.

- Clean solid **plastic toys** with three tablespoons of baking soda dissolved into a quart of warm water. Dip a sponge into the solution and rub it over the toys. Use a clean damp cloth to rinse.

- Baking soda can remove **crayon** from walls and even from launderable items. Place one-cup baking soda in the wash and run as usual. To remove crayon from walls, make a paste and scrub. Rinse with clean water. (Note: If the crayon doesn't come out of a fabric, wash it again before you place it in the drier, otherwise the heat could set the wax and color in for good.)

46

• Try adding a half a teaspoon of baking soda to a sink full of water and soak your **hair combs** and **brushes**. It will remove hair spray and oils in just a few minutes.

• Add a half-cup to your bath water to make your **skin softer** than it's ever been.

• For really **dirty gardener's hands**, a generous lump of baking soda mixed into a paste and scrubbed with a nailbrush will make your hands clean—and soft. The soil already makes a meal of your hands and cuticles, why should your hand soap, too?

- To boost your **laundry soap**, **soften** your **clothes** and deodorize an entire load of laundry, add one cup of baking soda to your automatic washing machine before adding your soap and clothes. Launder as usual.

- Keep your **cat box** smelling fresher by first sprinkling baking soda into the **litter box** before adding the cat litter.

- If your **dog** or **cat bedding** is less than fresh, sprinkle baking soda into it. Let it sit for about an hour and then vacuum.

- Add a half-cup of baking soda to a bucket of water and soak **cloth diapers** or even soiled

baby clothes to remove **odors**. Remove from this pre-wash and then launder as usual. The baking soda is safe enough even for use on items that will touch a newborn's skin.

• **Fill ashtrays** in your car and home to assist in absorbing odors and to make certain cigarettes are extinguished. (It's a filthy, nasty habit, but some folks still smoke!)

• For **oil** on your **driveway** or **garage floor**, sprinkle baking soda over the spots to absorb them. Add a bit of water to the baking soda to form a paste. With a brush in your hand or a scrub pad under the sole of your shoe, work it up. Rinse with soap and water, and repeat if necessary. It should get some of the spill or stains up. If not, get over it. It's a garage floor after all.

- Add a quarter of a cup to a bucket of water to remove **bugs** and **tree sap** from the **chrome**, **windshield glass**, **mud flaps**, **auto roof rack** and **auto-body paint** on your car. It's really effective as a scrub, too. Just apply a bit onto a rag or sponge to get the really nasty stuff up. Rinse with clean water. Try it on the **vinyl seats** inside, too.

- Sprinkle baking soda onto your upholstered **couch** or **favorite chair** to deodorize it. Let it stand for about an hour or so and then vacuum.

- Did you ever think that you could extinguish a **grease fire** with baking soda? It's true. (But let's hope you never have to put this to the test.)

• They may not be roses, but why shouldn't they smell like a dozen. Sprinkle a bit of baking soda into your **shoes** before and after wearing; **your feet** will feel cooled and your shoes will stay fresh.

• You're planning a cookout and your **outdoor grill** is a mess! Make a paste of baking soda and water and scrub with a wire brush to remove last night's (or last summer's!) remains. You'll need a bit of elbow grease to get it shiny. Rinse and repeat until clean.

• Sprinkle baking soda directly into your **garbage**. This will make it smell a lot fresher.

- Baked on messes are easy to remove simply by placing a couple of spoonfuls of baking soda and your dish liquid into the **bake pan**. Let it soak for an hour or, if necessary, overnight. Wipe it out with a cloth or a sponge. If any bits remain, make a baking soda paste and scrub the sticky bits right up. Rinse with clean water.

- Remove **coffee stains** and **tea stains** from your coffee pot, teapot and cups by scrubbing with baking soda and a soft cloth. Rinse with water.

- Your **sterling silver** or **silverplate** will always look like you have a full staff—even if all you have is a box of baking soda. (This is amazing.) Line your kitchen sink or a wash bucket with aluminum foil. (The heavy-duty stuff works best.) Load up the silver you intend to polish, making certain that each item touches the foil liner. Cover the entire contents with boiling water and add a cup of baking soda. The **tarnish** jumps from the silver to the foil in almost no time at all! For heavy tarnish that may still remain, make a paste of water and baking soda and polish the remaining surfaces 'til they shine.

- If you insist on using potentially toxic cleansers, after doing so, please clean all of your **kitchen surfaces** with baking soda to make certain that no cleaning chemicals end up in your food.

56

borax

ormed 18 to 20 million years ago, borax (Zen-Cleansing's second ingredient), is the fifth element on the periodic table of elements and lies buried deep in the Mohave Desert, the Andes, Turkey, Tibet and Death Valley. It forms in the most arid regions of the planet. Carried by streams flowing out from temporary lakes that accumulate during wet seasons from the runoff of nearby mountains, the mineral rich overflow becomes concentrated by evaporation in the scorched, barren, and dry desert climates. Ultimately the concentration builds to produce the crystals we know as borax.

For many of you, borax, like the then still young and ever-tanned face of Ronald Reagan, will forever be connected with the popular television show "Death Valley Days" (1952-1975). The weekly show about tales of the Old West was sponsored by 20 Mule Team Borax and presented by the Pacific Coast Borax Company.

Borax has a color that is white to clear, and its texture is fine and powdery, silky and smooth to the touch. Slightly soluble in cold water and highly soluble in hot, it can be used as a cleaning agent, weed killer, disinfectant or, as it says on the box, to "speed and sweeten laundry."

Store borax in the box it comes in or in a sealed recycled jar. Keep it in a dry place to keep the crystals light, soft and powdery.

Zen-Cleansing with Borax

• Adding one-quarter cup of borax to 2 cups water makes a highly effective **bleach substitute**. (Borax cleans and bleaches by converting some water molecules to hydrogen peroxide.)

• For **heavily soiled clothing**, add 1/2-cup borax to your detergent and launder clothes as usual.

No meal's complete until a garment's been soiled.

*Your tub and your spouse are the
ring bearers who know you best.*

- You may create a general, all-purpose **household cleaner** by adding one half of a cup of borax to one gallon of water.

- By combining equal parts borax and hot water, you create a highly effective **disinfectant**.

- Your **bathroom** will shine when cleaned with borax. Apply to a soft cloth or a dampened sponge and use as you would an ordinary bathroom **cleanser** or **kitchen cleanser**. It can be used on any surface in the bathroom or kitchen without the risk of scratching.

- Add one-quarter cup of borax to your **toilet bowl** to help clean and deodorize it. Swish the mixture with a brush and allow it stand for at least an hour or even better overnight. Then just flush.

- Borax is delicate enough for your **fine china** and **glassware** as well as **pots**, **pans** and **bakeware**. Add one half-cup to a sink full of water. Wash items well and rinse with clear water.

- Add one tablespoon of borax to one quart of warm water to clean and deodorize your **refrigerator**.

lemon

Introduction to Lemon

With sharp thorns and twigs, oblong leaves and fragrant buds of reddish hues that blossom into white and lavender flowers, the lemon fruit is light yellow, oval and aromatic. Dotted with oil glands that produce its memorable effervescent scent and hidden under the sun-ripened tough exterior of rind lies the lemon's acidic juicy segments. Pungent, sharp, heady, bitter, and at times overpowering, the perfect little citrus sections beneath the leathery exterior offer up what was once prized by sultans, gifted by kings, and traded across the continents by sailors, pirates and smugglers. Although its origin is unknown, the lemon is believed to have been cultivated in ancient Iraq and Egypt. It is rumored that Christopher Columbus carried its seeds in his vest pockets. Today the sour and succulent fruit is grown in Italy, Spain, Greece, Turkey, Cyprus, Lebanon, South Africa, Australia, the Philippines, and of course, the United States.

With names like Armstrong, Bearss, Berna, Eureka, Femminello Ovale, Genoa, Harvey, Interdonato, Lisbon, Meyer, Monachello, Nepali Oblong, Nepali Round, Perrine, Ponderosa, Rosenberger, Rough Lemon, Santa Teresa, Sweet Lemon, and Villafranca, the common lemon may not be "oh-so-common" after all. Lemons vary slightly in color, texture, shape, flavor and scent. Whether you choose the exotic or the mundane variety, any lemon you can get your hands on will certainly do the trick.

A bowl of a dozen placed casually out in the open, another bunch tossed into your refrigerator's crisper, and perhaps a small covered dish filled with cut pieces and slices ready for the taking stashed in your refrigerator door will make living with the most perishable of the five Zen-Cleansing ingredients that much easier.

Zen-Cleansing with Lemon

• Slice a lemon and put it into a pot of water and bring to a boil. After an hour the lemon **aroma** should most certainly refresh your home.

• Rub fresh lemon into a **cutting board** to remove discolorations. For heavy stains, allow it to sit. Wash and rinse with clear water.

• The juice of a lemon removes the **odor of onion or garlic** from **knives** and **hands**.

- Remove **berry stains** from your **hands** by placing a bit of lemon juice on them. Wash and rinse with clear water.

- Remove **ink stains** on cloth by placing lemon juice directly onto the spot. Allow to sit overnight before laundering as usual. Repeat if necessary before placing in the drier.

- To **brighten** your **white fabrics**, soak in a pot with boiling water and a sliced lemon.

- A 50-50 solution of lemon juice and water should dissolve your **hard water deposits**.

- To shine your **aluminum pots**, rub with the cut side of a lemon.

- To rid your **humidifier** of odors, add three or four caps of lemon juice to the water.

- Remove watermarks and grease from your **kitchen sink** after a big meal by adding a slice to your final rinse water.

salt

Introduction to Salt

Stored in shakers on dining tables, presented in heaping bowls, or found next to stovetops, this coarse, granular or powdery white element stands ready to offer the handy pinch to almost every sweet or savory culinary invention. Sprinkled over eggs, tossed over a frozen walkway, or used to cure meat, the plentiful common table salt can stand alone—(a pillar) among spices—and cleansers!

Listed on the periodic table of elements, sodium chloride in all its forms (iodized, sea, bay, kosher, canning, pickling or rock salt), occurs naturally in soil and water. Like baking soda, it too was used to preserve the remains of the ancient Pharaohs. Salt is the fourth most abundant element on earth, and it is even found in great bubbling lakes on the planet Mars.

No less than thirty references to salt are made in the Bible. (Most notably, perhaps, when Lot's wife was transformed into a cold and bloodless pillar of the stuff because she defiantly turned to see the fall of Gomorra.)

Roman soldiers of antiquity were often paid in salt, and this was called their salarium, from which our word "salary" is derived. It was said a soldier was "worth his salt," a term still used for a worthy person. Once paid with salt, it could be used as money in exchange for other goods.

Zen-Cleansing with Salt

- Clean your **wok** by scrubbing it clean with a small amount of salt on a paper towel dampened with cooking oil.

- In the event of an **oven spill**, sprinkle salt into the mess and then scrub.

- Remove **perspiration stains** in clothing by pre-soaking the garment in salt water.

There's no reason to cultivate mildew.
It doesn't bear fruit.

- Remove fresh **coffee stains** by dousing the affected area with cold salt water.

- Remove **bloodstains** in clothing by soaking the garment in cold salt water overnight. Wash as usual.

- Soak your laundered **shower curtain** in salt water. This should retard the growth of mildew.

- Salt and boiling water poured down your **drains** helps keeps them flowing.

- Salt will put out a **grease fire**.

- **Soften new jeans** by adding one half cup of salt and wash along with your regular laundry detergent.

- Remove **soapsuds** from your sink by adding salt to your rinse water.

- **Soap residue** is easily removed from your laundry by adding a quarter cup of salt to your rinse cycle. This also acts as a marvelous **fabric softener**, too.

- To erase **coffee stains** from the inside of a **glass coffee pot**, add 4 teaspoons salt, 1 cup crushed ice, and 1 tablespoon water. Gently swirl until clean, then rinse. Note: Coffee pot should be at room temperature before cleaning.

• Eliminate **odors** from of your **wooden cutting board** by applying a generous amount of salt directly on the board. Rub firmly with the palm of your hand. This should not only remove any odors but a bit of the surface grime as well. Rinse with water.

• Prevent runs in new **pantyhose**. Wash **pantyhose** and allow them to drip dry. Then mix two cups of salt with one gallon of water and soak pantyhose for three hours, rinse in cool water, and drip dry. This will make the hosiery stronger and less apt to run.

• Pour 1/2 cup of salt into the **garbage disposal**. Then, by running the disposal following manufacturer's directions, you'll send any odors down the drain!

• Use salt to help remove **wine stains** from cotton fabric. Pour enough salt on the stain to soak up the liquid. Soak the fabric for a half-hour in cold water. Wash as usual.

- Put your **silk flowers** into a large bag and pour in one cup of salt. Shake the contents. Your flowers are now clean.

- Pour a box of salt down your drain to prevent **frozen pipes** during winter months.

white vinegar

Introduction to White Vinegar

Sharp, sour and biting…rice, red, white, balsamic or apple cider. The flavor of vinegar, to most of us, always remains the same. But one to another is very different.

Vinegar, from the French meaning "sour wine," is produced from assorted fruits, berries, melons, coconut, honey, beer, maple syrup, potatoes, beets, malt, grains and whey. But the production in essence remains unaffected no matter what its origin— a first fermentation of sugar to alcohol, and then a second fermentation to vinegar. Viola! Acetic acid is born.

Most major religions make references to vinegar—whether it's Confucianism, Buddhism, Taoism or Christianity. In fact, when and how an immortal deity responded to the taste of vinegar was often used as a metaphor for that deity's view on life and its momentary circumstances.

The ancients stumbled upon the versatility of vinegar probably 10,000 years ago. The Babylonians used it as medicine and also flavored their meals with it. The Romans drank it as a beverage. Cleopatra dissolved pearls in it to prove she could devour a fortune in a single meal. Biblical references show how vinegar was used for its soothing and healing properties, and as recently as World War I, vinegar was still being used to treat wounds in the battlefields.

Susan B. Anthony was considered the "vinegar" of the Women's Suffrage movement. By being aggressive, breezy, ebullient, frisky, spunky and full of vitality, she displayed the classic traits of being full of "piss and vinegar," a phrase often used by Steinbeck in The Grapes of Wrath.

It's said, "You catch more flies with honey than with vinegar." So go ahead and clean with it. (Who wants to attract flies anyway?!) Store your white vinegar in a sealed container alone or dilute it 50/50 with water in a spray bottle for everyday use. There is no need for refrigeration. Vinegar's shelf life is eternal.

Zen-Cleansing with White Vinegar

•Always take a moment to recognize your materials and know your surfaces before you begin cleaning. A remarkable cleaner, white vinegar can cut **greasy film** but is strong enough to create pits and marks in marble. White vinegar is great for **colorfast clothes**… except for cotton and linen. Be sure to take a moment and read your content labels.

- White vinegar neutralizes alkaline soaps. It can remove **soap film** when added to your laundry's final rinse cycle.

- White vinegar also breaks down stubborn **urine odors.** Add a quarter of a cup to your washing machine when cleaning baby's diapers to make them soft and sweet—for the next "go-round."

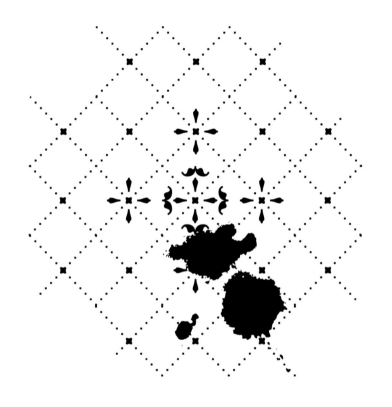

- You can polish **patent leather** using a cloth dampened with white vinegar. Just wipe it on full strength and gently rub and wipe off 'til the shine is fully restored.

- White vinegar works well as a **wallpaper remover**. Spray a mixture of half water/half vinegar and allow it to soak into the paper. Begin peeling, picking and scraping away.

- Remove **static cling** from your clothing by adding a quarter cup of white vinegar to the final rinse cycle in your washing machine.

• You can soften a hardened **paintbrush** by placing it in hot white vinegar. Place vinegar in a glass or plastic cup in the microwave (or in a pan on the stove top) and bring it to a slow boil. Remove it from the heat source and soak your paintbrushes in it overnight.

• When re-hemming clothes, sprinkle some white vinegar on the previous crease and iron over it. This will help take out the **pressing creases** to assist you in making a new hem.

• White vinegar unclogs the steam vents in an **electric iron**. Fill the reserve with vinegar and allow it to run full heat on the highest setting. Once the vents are clear, empty the iron of the excess white vinegar and refill with clean water.

• A solution of 2 tablespoons of white vinegar to one gallon of warm water in a spray bottle is great way to clean **mirrors**, **glass** and **windows**. Spray onto the area to be cleaned and polish with recycled newspapers.

• Dilute one cup of white vinegar with one cup of room temperature water to reduce the **odor** of a **pet's urine** in your **carpeting**. Apply and blot with a clean cloth or rag.

• Fill a spray bottle with a half-and-half mixture of water and white vinegar to **deodorize** the air while you are cooking. Spritz it around and notice the difference.

• Fill a bathtub with super hot water and add a cup of white vinegar. By hanging your clothes in the white vinegar infused steam, **smoke** and **other odors** can be reduced.

• Keep your car windows frost-free with a homemade **defroster**. Coat the windshield and windows the night before with a solution of three parts white vinegar to one part water. (Don't wipe it off.) It's also a great way to clean your **car windows**.

• Polish your cars' auto **body chrome** by applying white vinegar full strength with a soft cloth. Buff until it's shiny.

95

• Remove **skunk odor** from your dog. Rub Fido's fur with full strength white vinegar and then bathe as usual. "Rinse and repeat" may well apply in this situation. (You'll probably need a bath, too, when you're done!)

• To **deodorize your kitchen drain**, pour a cup of white vinegar down the drain once a week. Let stand 30 minutes and then flush with cold water.

- Eliminate onion and garlic odors from your **hands** and from your **knives** and **kitchen surfaces** by rubbing white vinegar on everything before and after slicing.

- Clean and disinfect your **wooden cutting boards** by wiping with full-strength white vinegar.

- To remove **fruit stains** from hands simply rinse with white vinegar.

- Cut through grease and odor on your **dishes** by adding a tablespoon of white vinegar to hot soapy wash water. Rinse with clean water.

98

• To clean a stained and soiled **teapot**, boil a half-and-half mixture of water and white vinegar in the teapot over a high flame on your stove. Bring it to a full boil. Dispose of the mixture and then wipe away the grime with a rag.

• Wash out your **refrigerator** with a solution of equal parts water and white vinegar. It will make everything sparkle.

• Clean and deodorize your **garbage disposal** by making white vinegar ice cubes. Feed enough cubes to fill the disposal and then operate. After grinding, run cold water through to rinse it clean.

- To clean your **dishwasher**, place a cup of white vinegar into the bottom of the appliance and operate through an entire cycle. Do this once a month to reduce soap build up on the inner rollers, racks gaskets and sprayers.

- By wiping with a white vinegar dampened cloth. Safely clean and shine **stainless steel** around your home and in your kitchen.

- Add a cup of white vinegar to a sink of warm water to clean **fine china**, **crystal** and **glassware**. Dip the item in the solution, rinse with warm water and allow to air dry.

- To get stains and baked on "ick" out of **pots** and **pans**, fill the offending receptacle with 3 tablespoons of white vinegar and a pint of water. Allow the mixture to boil on your stovetop until the stain or "goo" loosens. Pour the mixture down the drain and then wash the rest away with soap and water.

- Boil 1/4 cup of white vinegar and 1 cup of water in a glass or plastic container in your **microwave** for two minutes. The condensation from the boiling mixture will loosen splattered-on-food and those mysterious cheesy lumps, and will even deodorize the machine in the process. Wipe the inside clean with a damp cloth or sponge.

• Periodically, pour a cup of white vinegar into your **washing machine.** Allow it to operate through a regular cycle with no clothes added. This will dissolve soap residue from the drum of your machine and will keep it running smoothly for years.

• To prevent greasy **oven** buildup in the first place, dip a sponge in full-strength white vinegar and wipe down all sides of the **oven,** inside and out.

• Stop unpleasant **cooking odors** from permeating throughout your house. Simply boil two cups of white vinegar in a pot on the stovetop. The vinegar will absorb the offending odors.

103

- Soak a towel in white vinegar. Wring it out and swing it around the room to remove the odor of **smoke** from the air. This works for smoke from tobacco as well as badly burned toast!

- To clean an automatic drip **coffee maker**, run full-strength white vinegar through a normal brew cycle. Rinse by running plain water through the cycle twice. The pot will be remarkably clean and your coffee will taste better than ever. (Tip: Coffee sometimes tastes bitter because of soapy residue; therefore never wash your pot with soap.)

• Scour your **bathroom sink** and **tub** with full-strength white vinegar. Apply it with a sponge or a cloth and wipe it clean. It will remove that ugly **soap scum** ring.

• Clean your **ceramic tiles** with a solution of 1/4-cup white vinegar to one-gallon warm water. Expect a miraculous shine.

• To remove **hard water spots** on your **tub**, **shower doors** and **shower stall**, apply full-strength white vinegar, wipe, let stand for five minutes then rinse with clean water. It will look as good as new.

- Clean up accidentally **spilled white glue** with white vinegar.

- **Deodorize your car** by soaking a piece of bread in white vinegar. Place it on a bowl or a plate and leave it in the car overnight.

- Soak your rusty **tools** in white vinegar for a few hours or overnight. If needed, change the vinegar as it becomes cloudy.

- To remove **grass stains**, mix one-third cup white vinegar and two-thirds cup water. Apply the solution to the stain and blot with a clean cloth. Repeat the process, as needed, then wash as usual.

- Keep **lint** from clinging to your dark clothes by adding 1/2-cup white vinegar to the rinse cycle. (Remember to check for colorfast and fiber content first!)

- Use white vinegar to get rid of the **hard water deposits** around your sink. Soak a clean cloth with white vinegar and place it around the area that needs to be cleaned. Allow it to sit overnight. Rinse and wipe clean.

- Get your **grout** clean with full-strength white vinegar. Scrub with a toothbrush. (This sounds kind of obsessive but it works.)

- Two drops of white vinegar in your laundry will keep your **colors nice and bright**. (Relax, just two drops aren't gonna' hurt anything.)

- Add a quarter cup of white vinegar to rinse water to remove soapy or oily film from **laminate**, **Formica surfaces** or **Corian counters**. (Keep in mind vinegar will create pits in "real" marble surfaces.)

• Rinse **jars** and **containers** with white vinegar to eliminate odors of previous contents.

• When rinsing dishes in a sinkful of hot water, add a cap full of white vinegar to your rinse water to cut **grease** or **excess soap**. Your dishes will sparkle.

• Eliminate the smell of **cigarettes** or **paint** by placing a small bowl of white vinegar in a room. Leave it overnight and replace it the next day if needed.

- Fill a spray bottle with white vinegar to chase away **ants**. They hate it.

- Remove **salt stains** from your shoes by wiping them with equal parts white vinegar and water.

- Get rid of **deodorant** and **antiperspirant residue** on washables by lightly rubbing the spots with white vinegar before washing. (Again, check labels for content and colorfastness.)

- Unclog any soap scum formations from your **washing machine** by pouring a gallon of white vinegar into the washer tub and running it full cycle.

• After washing a **wool sweater** by hand, rinse one-quarter cup of white vinegar and a sink of water to remove any additional odors. Rinse with clean water.

• Pour white vinegar on any **unwanted grasses** (or **weeds**) for their swift elimination, especially in crevices and in between bricks.

• Clean **plastic** and **cloth shower curtains** in the washing machine. Add one cup of white vinegar to the rinse cycle to help deter mold and mildew.

Potions, inventions and concoctions...a pinch of this and that. When mixing any of the fab-five Zen-Cleansing ingredients (baking soda, borax, lemon, salt, vinegar) you create a recipe for a wholesome, healthy and natural clean.

Shakespeare wrote of potions made and potions offered to miraculous and consequential effect. You, too, can expect a bit of magic--bubbles rising and cloudy swirling waters--while you clean. Channel the witches of Macbeth while you rinse a pot, wash the floor, or scrub your tub. Become a Mary Magdalene, a Mr. Belvedere, a Hazel or Mr. French by purifying your home with baptismal zeal. Pretend you're the Iron Chef, the Naked Chef, or the Domestic Goddess of the household arts. And always remember to take pride in your magical (and sometimes muscular) power to clean.

Allow the preparations that follow to become your personal springboard for thoughtful cleaning creativity. Since the fab-five ingredients are harmless, use these proven recipes and potions to create your own Zen-Cleansing arsenal.

Some Basic Zen-Cleansing Recipes

• Equal parts of borax, baking soda and ivory soap flakes makes amazing **laundry soap**. Store in a sealed glass jar. You'll never use anything else.

• To unclog a **drain**, pour a handful of baking soda down the drain and add 1/2 cup of white vinegar. Rinse with hot water.

• Replace your electric **dishwashing soap** with equal parts baking soda and borax. By adding just a splash of vinegar in the rinse cycle your stemware and glasses are certain to be extra shiny.

• Two parts olive oil mixed with one part lemon juice will make great **furniture polish**. Just a few drops on a soft cloth will get your wood furniture to shine. Store in a glass jar.

- Clean your oven without caustic or dangerous chemicals by sprinkling its cooled interior with baking soda and then applying lemon juice. Watch the **oven cleaner** bubble and let it sit for an hour. Clean with fresh water and a cloth.

- By cleaning with equal parts baking soda and white vinegar, your **toilet bowl** will be fresh and clean.

- To add to the longevity of fresh cut **flowers**, add 2 tablespoons white vinegar and 1-teaspoon sugar for each quart of water.

- Remove fish, garlic or onion **odor** from your **hands** by rubbing with a lemon wedge dipped in salt, and then rinse with water.

• Remove **mineral deposits** and **debris** from a **glass flower vase** by mixing 1/3-cup salt and 2 tablespoons white vinegar to form a paste. Apply to inside of vase and let it stand 20 minutes then scrub. Rinse vase and dry.

• Clear the air with a homemade **air freshener.** Just cut a lemon in half, remove pulp, and fill the peel with salt. It will provide a pleasant, aromatic lemon-y scent anywhere in your home.

• **Remove rust** from household tools and chrome by using salt and one tablespoon of lemon juice. Create a paste and apply to the rusted area with a dry cloth and rub.

- Mix one-quarter cup borax and one-quarter cup baking soda to make the best **bath cleaner** and **kitchen cleaner** ever. Add some salt as an abrasive if necessary.

- To remove stains on your **Formica counter** tops, squeeze fresh lemon juice on the spot and let it sit for 30 minutes. Sprinkle with baking soda, then scrub with a sponge. Rinse with clean water and wipe dry.

- Eliminate smelly odors from your **chopping block** by sprinkling on baking soda and then adding white vinegar. Let the two sizzle and bubble, then rinse clean. This is also a swell way to clean your sink and tub.

- Make a baking soda and water paste and rub it onto soiled or stained collars and armpits before washing as a **laundering pre-wash**. Add a little white vinegar to stubborn stains (and check for colorfast/fabric content). Follow by washing as usual.

- For a fresh **deodorized refrigerator**, leave an open box of baking soda or even a bowl of cut lemons on the shelf.

- Odor from **fires** are difficult. You may wash your walls and surfaces with a mixture of white vinegar and lemon diluted in water. Wash any clothing that is smoke damaged five times (yes, I said five) and adding one-half cup each of white vinegar and baking soda to the rinse cycle every time.

- Sprinkle baking soda on whatever **surface** you want to clean. Next, add white vinegar to the soda. If you need to make it more powerful, just add a little borax.

- To remove **mildew** from just about anything, use equal parts white vinegar and borax.

- To make an **all-purpose liquid cleaner**, combine equal amounts of white vinegar and borax.

- For stubborn **bath stains** or **kitchen stains**, clean surfaces by using a mixture of lemon juice and borax. Scrub it with an abrasive pad. Rinse with clean water.

- For stains on either **porcelain** dishes or bath and **kitchen fixtures**, rub a sliced lemon dipped into salt to remove the stains.

- To whiten **yellowed cotton** and **linen fabrics** add ¼ cup each of baking soda and salt to your largest enamel pot filled with water. Boil under a watchful eye for about an hour.

- You may dip half a lemon into borax to create a **basin, tub** and **tile cleaner**. Scrub using the halved lemon, juicy side down. Rinse with clean water.

- Lemon juice or salt makes a good **spot remover**.

- To clean a **non-coated pan** of a burnt-on mess, boil a mixture of equal parts white vinegar and baking soda right in the pan.

- Polish **copper pans** with a half a lemon dipped into salt. Rub in a circular motion and then rinse in clear water. Repeat until the copper shines. (A mix of vinegar and salt also works well.)

- To clean your **brass**, make a paste with equal parts white vinegar, flour and salt. Leave on for an hour and then buff with soft cloth.

- To get pesky, persistent **tomato stains** (or stains from spices, herbs, etc.) out of your **plastic storage containers**, scrub them using multiple combinations of lemon juice, baking soda and white vinegar. (Note: Elbow grease required, and this one ain't guaranteed! Remember—it isn't your family heirloom china.)

. . . .

Live life to the fullest. Respect the physical…be in the moment.

1. Clean a little every day….the best way to devour an elephant is by eating it one slow bite at a time.

2. There's no reason to clean alone. Drag a lover, neighbor, spouse, child, parent or pet into the act. It's always better with two.

3. Anybody can clean. (No excuses.)

4. Clean with thoughtful consideration and significance. Lose yourself in the ordinary, and by doing so infuse it with meaning.

5. Not everything needs cleaning. A little (very little) grime can sometimes be swell.

6. Prioritize. If a must-see movie, short-lived play, or an exhibition or concert recital stands between you and clean living, opt for culture.

7. At a certain point, any space can only get so dirty—don't obsess. So if your schedule doesn't allow you to clean weekly, then do it bi-monthly. In the scheme of things, nobody will really notice the difference.

8. Your home is a reflection of who you are. It's a gift to those around you each time you care to plan, organize, entertain, cook and clean.

9. For every action there's a reaction. When you clean, expect something marvelous in return.

10. Fix it, change it, clean it, make it better or get rid of it.

11. Why clean? Why ask?